THE TIMEKEEPER

A POETIC EXPLORATION OF TIME HOPE & HUMAN EXISTENCE

AMY CECILIA GRAINGER

THE TIMEKEEPER

AMY CECILIA GRAINGER

©2025 Amy Cecilia Grainger
All rights reserved.

First published 2025

No part of this publication may be reproduced, stored in a retrieval system, or transmitted in any form or by any means—electronic, mechanical, photocopying, recording, or otherwise—without prior written permission of the author.

Disclaimer:
This work reflects the author's philosophical inquiry and lived experience. It is intended for personal reflection and creative exploration only and does not constitute professional advice or instruction. Readers remain solely responsible for their own interpretations and actions.

Author:
Amy Cecilia Grainger

Published by
Souls of Ones Feet

Graphic Design & Cover:
Ged L. M. Buick
ISBN: 978-1-0683830-0-7

:

'Time has gifted me many things,
yet, nothing quite like the connection's'

Mechanical time holds stability
Structures through systems
Restricting the flow of natures - universal unpredictables

THE EVER EXPANDING NOW

BEGINNING
In the beginning there was dust, molecules and magic; a dance so tragic, a collision, composure, a new world grows older – the beginning – kept expanding – and now – times is not withstanding.

BRIDGE
Feel this book as a gift, a journey of from my heart to yours. A bridge.

Release any expectations.

Allow yourself to travel – to unravel – to evolve and to explore!

BEACON
Allow the words of these explorations to illuminate the avenues of your time.

Feel love, feel peace, feel hope in your heart.

Be time.

BACK TO A BEGINNING
When we evolve time disintegrates - we uncover a space often reserved or overlooked - time does not end.

It infinitely- begins again.

CONTENT

THE EVER-EXPANDING NOW..7
MESSAGE FROM THE AUTHOR 11
INSPIRATION SURROUNDS US 14
ORIGIN OF THE TIMEKEEPER...19

FLOW ONE 26
FLOW TWO 30
FLOW THREE...34
FLOW FOUR..38
FLOW FIVE 42
FLOW SIX..46

FLOW SEVEN..50
FLOW EIGHT...54
FLOW NINE...58
FLOW TEN..62
FLOW ELEVEN 66
FLOW TWELVE...68

POETIC EXTENSION INTRO................................73
A LEGACY...76
MORE IN THIS SERIES..79
INVITATION TO EXPLORE FURTHER.............82

"I recollect time in it's passing
The memories making and massing
The joining and motion of time in commotion
Is my one true passion"

MESSAGE FROM THE AUTHOR

HOW DOES IT FEEL TO BE HUMAN?

Welcome to this poetic series, which offers an alternative way to examine a philosophy of hope - a philosophy I refer to as the Souls of One's Feet.

This journey began long before I could grasp the depth of its significance. Now, after much turbulence and many transitions, I bring my philosophy to life. Like all human explorations this is going to be turbulent maybe a little uncomfortable.

Souls of One's Feet is about what carries us when nothing else does - a lifelong invitation to hold hope; a vibration that has been at the heart of my musings for over two decades. For me an exploration on what it means to be human.

After much deliberation, observation and exploration, I have concluded that for me, being human is a journey of hope. Over time, I have mused in meanders mapping a poetic series that serve as a bridge to my philosophy. This bridge begins with The Timekeeper... although you may read any of my works in an order you choose...In remembrance that we all arrive in our own space - in time.

Throughout our human journey, we navigate endless avenues of emotion. We seek a middle ground - a harmonious balance - we never quite land in this space, not until we leave this earthly place.

What exactly are we searching for?

Why are we here?

What does it mean to be human?

There exists an empty space I refer to as the 'middle-way' . This is the space, where we pause. The space we feel between our humans experience. These pauses form, what I describe as sequences; sequences I map through my time.

In my observations, hope expands mostly in the sequences of joy. Rarely is it remarked upon in the quieter, more subtle sequences of discomfort. As human beings we dance through light and dark. Through the ebb and flow we call life, we are the dance of existence in time.

Each human experiences time that challenges them, a happening that changes the structure of reality. A loss, a trauma, a profound shift in how it feels to be human. These moments create ripples in frequencies that move through us. If they feel uncomfortable we may avoid-dance. We are always - dancing.

The purpose of these poetic explorations is to illuminate the sequences of hope and formulate a bridge to my life's work a philosophy that comes from my heart. To experience my musings in the hope that is intended I invite you to feel time and space in a way that may appear unusual, uncomfortable, or even uncertain. In this discomfort time expands. Uncertainty deepens our awareness of time, in these spaces we may examine layers of our existence through a lens of hope.

hope

INSPIRATION SURROUNDS US

Time does not tick solely from the hands of a clock - it pulses in the hush between heartbeats, it stretches across the shadow of a tree at dusk, and folds itself into the corners of our memory, until our memory is no more. The timekeeper is born from these delicate pathways and the spaces between which you may here me refer to 'asleep - awake - asleep - awake.

Time is not separate from us; it is us - etched into the laugh lines of a stranger, whispered in the rustle of the leaves, mirrored in the moonlight; time radiates through the suns beams, reminding us with softness all that hope may be.

This book is a map through time's many dimensions - a collection of pauses, awakenings, and quiet reckonings. These poems are not only words, but extractions of presence sometimes through absence, a reminder that hopes inspiration is never far. It is the breath in your lungs, the silence after a goodbye, the rhythm of all things born, then lost. You are the timekeeper - and everything around you is keeping time with-in you.

Read along with me on my poetry channel.
Let's journey together through the verses, allowing the words
to resonate and unfold.

www.soulsofonesfeet.bandcamp.com

THE ORIGINS OF THE TIMEKEEPER

SOULS OF ONES FEET
A PHILOSOPHY OF HOPE

During meditation at a sacred sojourn, I was gifted the name The Timekeeper. At first, I didn't know what to make of it. I felt a wave of excitement, followed by overwhelming confusion. Had I heard this before, had I invented it myself? The name felt strange, like something I had known but never fully acknowledged. Yet, in the stillness of a passing moment, I felt a sense of quiet affirmation; *'I am the timekeeper - I travel through dreams that disperse...'* What did it mean - was the pulsing question of my heart.

It was not the name itself that mattered so much, but the reminder of what it represented, the vibration in the bellow, the elegance in thee echo, as time passed, as my heart grasped, the meaning in this feeling - something new emerged...ME.

The Timekeeper was an invitation, not a title. It was an acknowledgement of the spaces I occupy and the time I explore. This title spoke not of ownership but of observation – of existing within the ebb and flow of time, of being both participant and witness to existence. In this quiet revelation, I realised that time and space are not separate entities, but intertwined in a dance that defines our human experience. Time moves through us, shaping and reshaping our lives, while we, in turn, shape it with every choice, every heartbeat – while in a middleway the universe echoes affirmations of love and hope.

This was not the beginning of my journey but it felt like once again I was back to a beginning. My acknowledgement was that until this point I had never fully validated my purpose or passions within myself. Instead, I sought others to listen, to feel, and to acknowledge for me. I lacked confidence, feeling unlovable and unworthy, as ancestral traumas reverberated through my being. And then, I heard a whisper, *'I am the timekeeper - I travel through dreams that disperse...'*

In the work that follows, I offer a poetic exploration of twelve unique philosophical flows about time. Each piece reflects the rhythms of existence, from the pauses between moments to the rush of change. It is a journey through time, a way of examining how we move within it and how it moves within us. These spaces are filled with moments of stillness, of expansion, and contraction. They are filled with vibrations of hope.

The Timekeeper is not a title I claim for myself. It is a role we all play. We are all timekeepers, navigating the sacred flow of life, marking the spaces and moments that define our existence. I invite you to journey with me through this exploration, to reflect, to question, what it means to be – a human being – keeping time.

Every moment is both fleeting and eternal.
Feel through your heart space,
the time that your faith does grace.

Who are you?

How did you arrive?

The hope that you are holding is the hope that gifts you life.

FLOW ONE

Many may ask who I am
Who I think I am maybe not
As I stand within raw awareness
I am up against a clock

A mechanical meader
     A middleway messiah
Not religion, nor jargon nor junk

Being human

     Being human

It's time to recalibrate and debunk

I am me in many ways
Yet, I will never – be you
Not in essence nor in clarity
A dance between many and few

Alignment – Alignment
Time vibrates a new assignment

That when we separate - the space
Where time it falls between
There is a heart within an avenue
A gift of light full beam
Yet, there is only you who may touch it
Only you who may feel
The essence in your being
     Through your being human—ideal

We humans dance and we jolly
We objectify as we fill these trolley's

The shops, the surplus
The waste is a waste of purpose

Time

       Time

Gently intertwined

I refer to my being as a Timekeeper
Observing through the pathways we wend

I invite YOU on this journey

Where love is thee evolving trend

FLOW TWO

I am the Timekeeper
I travel through dreams that disperse
I hold hope in harmony's rhythm

I am life

    I am death

I am birth

I recollect time in it's passing

The memories making and massing

The joining and motion of time in commotion
Is my one true passion

I observe grace with gratitude
Through all I have been and have seen
As day passes to night

I am whole

    I am love

I am light

I speak of time forgotten
I recall time that was not
Yet the synchronicities that mellows
As the clock chime bellows
Remind me of times I had forgot

The melody that rings
        The anchor that persists
Breathes space into time
    In all that one resists

I am the Timekeeper
I travel through dreams that disperse
I hold hope in harmony's rhythm

I am life

      I am death

I am birth

While my knowing in my being- echoes
Time stands still
This is where we hold
The trajectories that have been
We release and we respond
We embark and we embrace
In our embodied understanding
We are one
    We are love
We are grace

Mechanical time holds stability
Structures through systems
Restricting the flow of natures - universal unpredictables
How far do we fall
    How far do we go
Through the timeless impossibilities
Of all we do and do not know

I will leave this motion for you
To place in a time that you choose
Set your open heart with intention

Breathe love

        Breathe time

 Breathe through

I am the timekeeper
I travel through dreams that disperse
I hold hope in harmony's rhythm

I am love

        A life

Rebirthed

FLOW THREE

I open the doors, I anchor the gates
        of the fortress that timelessness creates
I flow through this middleway
Time it holds my hand
Now, I offer you a gentle space
To reflect without command

Breathe

    Flow to a pace that you set
There is no greater awareness
    Than a beat that is about to reset

I am the Timekeeper
I am an anchor in extremities
I am the tail before the wind
    The hyper Inocular currencies
I am blood and skin unveiled
I am human
I feel and hold my space
I leave before I arrive
Disembark through a middleway
Where we live before we die

I am the Timekeeper
I am an anchor in extremities
The sun before the light
The rays before the flow
As the waves curtail effortlessly
I am a gentle distant glow

A reminder
The voice between the sand

As the grains of dust they fall
Eloquently through your hand

Flow
      Flow

Breath as you go
Meander through in feeling
Of a time not so forth revealing
Hidden in the hallways
The memos in the meaning

I am the Timekeeper
I am an anchor in extremities
The Moon before the stars
The universe in all its wars

I am light

      I am dark

I am human

I flow with an open heart
Gifting time in allurance

With a beating end -
                - Restart

I speak of time forgotten
I recall time that was not
Yet the synchronicities that mellows
As the clock chime bellows
Remind me of times I had forgot

FLOW FOUR

There is a space that twists and turns
Geometrically confirms
That nature aligns unmechanically
Bridging space through its eloquent terms

Love,
    Hope and harmony

Alignment entropically
To soothe a world from catastrophe

We unravel from a beginning
A time set to end
    A human understanding
A universal blend
    An ambiguous corridor
A stairway sets the trend

Spirals
    Spirals

Dictations and digital virals

Spirals
    Spirals

    Breathe

I am the Timekeeper
I travel through dreams that disperse
To set space to a time held in motion
Not a space held in reverse

We meander
 We meander
We diligently pander
To the clock - to the cogs
To this mechanical extravaganza

I am the Timekeeper
I am hear to help you align
To heal through a space once a motion
A space to eloquently shine

Breathe -

Flow at a pace that you choose
There is no better calibrated concoction
Than an awareness - to which you amuse
Your human understanding
The deliberated demanding
The pause through an avenue
Where you are the Captain
You are the one who is commanding

I am the Timekeeper
I am an anchor in extremities
The wave as it ripples in space
Crashing to bring you deliverance
Only if you set the pace

FLOW FIVE

The purpose to this exploration
Is to realign misinterpretation
Of what being human does mean
An investigation of time
An avenue sublime

I am back to a beginning
As the sequences they seep
Through time in all its glory
And - the power humans seek
Fame is not in the money
Nor the paper it is printed on
It is not the time that did not land
For, by—gone,

                By—gone

I am the Timekeeper
I have placed my container down
If only to meet in a middleway
Unacknowledged—unheard—and unfound
A diluted discrepancy
A pathway uncommonly wend
A timeless hypocrisy
Where fear does label the trend

Let us step out of this middleway
Where jargon is frequently strewn
To, open our heart to a hopeful space
Where love - begins to bloom
We could recap the time that was
We may consider what may be
And ask, why are we still forging wars
On land and overseas

Change is not in the ocean, nor rock, nor sediment
It is held within our human hearts
Love gifts us - sentiment
Yet, humans still go hungry
Our youth are traumatised
The earth is breaking down
Should we open our eyes
In hope that when the heart does see

                                        Time will synchronise

FLOW SIX

I am the Timekeeper
A label nothing more
That extracts how I evolved
Through times passion - as is now was before
Patience - patience
Echoes through vibrations felt
While anchored in a middleway
Where fear begins to melt

I will arrive in the space my heart envisions
Through the feeling of believing
That flows through hopeful rivers
That gifts meaning to being - truth for seeing
Time -
Gentle time - holding everything worth 'being'

Hold love

   Hold time

Hold your heart most divine
Listen—
       Listen
Feel - the flow of time

Time matters not for objects
That disintegrate to dissolve
It eloquently meanders as it echoes

Evolve

    Evolve

        Evolve

I am the Timekeeper
A label gifted through time in passing
A dance within a middleway
Where the light ways are elusively crashing

Listen
    Feel
Open your heart to reveal
The space within your middleway
The flow that sets your pace

Recalibrate
        Reinvigorate
Your sanctuary
        Your space

I am back to a beginning
As the sequences they seep
Through time in all its glory
And the power humans seek

FLOW SEVEN

We flow through ambiguity
From the moment we arrive
A timeless misinformed malignancy
 - *to toc* - is to survive

We arrive - in an expectant mechanical meander
Where the feeling in your heart
Radiates with grandeur

Beat

  Beat

  Bellow and repeat

I am the Timekeeper
A label that drifts through space
To describe how I meander
Within my human grace

Tic toc -

     Tic toc -

There is hope held within my pace
In recognition, and acknowledgement
That time does not shrink nor swell
It barely barters reasoning
Nor does time it tell
Of the harrows or the sorrows
           Of the realigned cahoot
The trajectories, the jargon
    Our world is on reboot

Mechanical meanderance
Societal adherence
Digital dominance

I am the Timekeeper
I am here to help you embrace
The love within your heart
That patiently holds grace
A space no more human than before
Yet every-time you visit
There is more space - to explore

You see,
Expectations fall between
The avenues of time
Before we arrive
Eloquence does align
We choose to feel
We choose to hold our heart
In a way that realigns the jargon

To release is to embark
On a journey quite ambiguous
Elusive to say the least
An open heart is the only way
To hold on - yet release
Time we may know
Not time we once knew
For this dance is a magnificent meanderance
Of universal love at its grandest

FLOW EIGHT

I acknowledge the beginning
The time before the end
As time flows in a knowing
            that only time may wend

Love lands in feeling's
        Where we place hope into believing

Through the light waves

            Through the avenues

We expand and we evolve

We acknowledge what it means to be human
We adventure far beyond
Let us travel gently - hold humanity's hand
As I guide within this middleway
    with the hope to make a difference
            Wherever my feet land

Let us acknowledge the beginning
The time before the end
Where time flows in a knowing
That only time may wend
An arrival through a spiral
In all the time we feel
Whether we are walking
If we stand or sit or kneel
All that is above us
All that we embark
Is a journey - in discovery
A meander - both light and dark

I acknowledge the beginning
The space my heart returns
Where I contemplate compassionatly
The time before the end
To hold space in a middleway
Where hope sets time in trend

Here I am
        The Timekeeper
Holding the space within my view
To unravel through your purpose
What being human means for you

FLOW NINE

I am the Timekeeper
I am a vision beyond despair
Anchored in time through a middleway
I am weightless - beyond repair
I recollect time in its passing
The breathing is heavily massing
As the feet burn to bare
The space that is rare
I am the Timekeeper

Here
                  Yet there

There is a flow within a frequency
Where time is felt in feeling

Breathing
    Revealing

Anchored to a space one is leaving

Release
    Release

Release the space that burdens

That holds captive the life giving organs

Release
 Recalibrate
   Rejuvenate

Now is your time

To stand in the house of humanity
Divine
     Divine
 Divine
I am the Timekeeper
I am a vision beyond despair
To open your heart to a central space
To gift healing
To softly repair
The structure in the sanctuary
The sequence held in time
Where love flows through a hopeful space

               A heart that's held in time

We flow through ambiguity
From the moment we arrive
A timeless misinformed malignancy
—to toc— is to survive

FLOW TEN

There is a space that flows through a middleway
A meander held and anchored
That encapsulates beauty with grace
Through all that time encounters
When we sit
       When we pause
When we close our eyes and open our heart

There is a breathless hesitation
     A rotation in kickstart
I am the Timekeeper
    I am a vision beyond despair
Anchored through hope in a middle
A commune of love - graced elsewhere

You see,
There are these flows

These episode's -
  That fall in sequence through time

Where we map the hope and the love
Captured in little things like a smile
Time it dances with eloquence
Through the echoes that fall into space
When we listen
 Only listen
To the space where one does find grace

Breathe

    Breathe

Release

Feel time - now feel at ease
I am the Timekeeper
I am a space that is safe and abundant
Guided by fortune in energy
Not materials that catastrophically - fluctuate
My love radiates beyond avenues
Where darkness greets light in acceptance
Now it's time to step forth
Shed forgiveness through every repentance
No human is perfect
No time can escape this grip
Of existence as it disintegrates
Like a clock that mechanically ticks

FLOW ELEVEN

Round and round the avenues
Round and round the face
One to twelve in numbers
A cycle - disseminates
The orders and the rituals
The mechanical numerical mysticals
That dance from - sunrise to sunset
To breathe as time gently - resets

The rhythm in the motion
The pace within the purpose
As the passion falls between
All that lands to surface

I am the Timekeeper
An embodiment of being in my prime
A label that channels to align
The confusion in catastrophe
The fire felt in fear
The rising of the rivers as anxiety creeps near

Labels
        Expressions
                Experiences
Landing through time
External interactions
From an internal viral - line
As the whisper waves so softly
From the wind - it wend - divine

FLOW TWELVE

The beginning grants acceptance
While the ending does draw near
For a Timekeeper can only keep the time
 While they are *'here'*
There or here could be anywhere-
Any space in any time
Which is the hope of this bridge
To poetically re-align

The dimensions in the middleway
Where love falls down to fear
As the hope it hides in hindrance
Of the darkness that draws near
Eventually it radiates as patiently it waited
For the light to find the avenue - unanticipated

Acknowledgement

        Acceptance

A landing in love where one wends

Deep into timelessness

        A beginning where hope knows no end

Time it dances with eloquence
Through the echoes that fall into space
When we listen
Only listen
To the space where one does find grace

GRATITUDE & LOVE LIVE HERE

A LEGACY

POETIC EXTENSION

As we come to the end of *The Timekeeper*, I offer you a poetic extension titled; '*A Legacy*'. This flow stands apart from the twelve explorations that precede it, while remaining intrinsically connected to the themes and philosophy that guide my journey. While the main poems invites you to reflect on time, human existence, and hope, *A Legacy* seeks to encapsulate the essence of what we leave behind as we move through these cycles - of time and hope.

The legacy we leave is not simply a imprint on space, it is an intangible energy bound with love, hope and wisdom, a space that continue to ripple through the lives of those we touch.

This additional flow serves as a reminder of the power of a legacy, not in the material sense, but in the way we affect others, how we share our energy, how we contribute to the collective soul of humanity. We all leave behind something meaningful. Through this exploration, I invite you to consider the kind of legacy you wish to create.

In this final flow, I aim to honour the journey we have taken together throughout The Timekeeper, while simultaneously inviting you to look beyond time itself. What stories will be told of you? What legacy will you leave to future generations? How can we ensure that the legacy of hope, peace, and love continues to ripple forward, long after we are gone?

A LEGACY

There is a legacy
An abundant, apprehended discrepancy
That falls down - when we lean over
For the anchor at weight
Can't quite disseminate
The space that's required nor time
When we listen is where we align

A Hopeful fragmented philosophy
Each setting and stage - transponding
Reflecting how one is responding
To the feelings and flows of being human

To connect

    To create

Through the vale of search and synchronicity
Through the space where we humans evolve
Where I am you - and you are me-
Together - In this legacy
Woven in space
    Held in time -
Generations anchored and primed
Expectations - deliberations
When hope - one does hold
The bridge does collapse and fold
There is an anchor in the middle way
A space where love does shine
Beyond judgement and fear

Beyond the...... Mine
    Mine

Mine

    A legacy -
A hopeful embodied philosophy
Interconnected avenues
That flow from before we knew when
The vibrations of all one desires
Are not here - or there - or then
They reside in the moment that was
Captured, through times trepid flaws
The mishaps and the middleway
The laughter and the joys
The togetherness
Not foreverness
An interconnected space - we deploy

Time in its most abundant
Not aberrant, nor questioned, nor feared
A hallway or a corridor
Where compassion is a pathway well steered

A legacy

A hopeful peaceful philosophy
The modern world is collapsing
Formulating a new time in space
 - the only one to survive
One we will gift to our children
When our departure will finally arrive
Thus I ask—
Should we now flow together?
Hold open our hearts and minds
To re-energise this world of ours
Through a legacy of hope that now shines

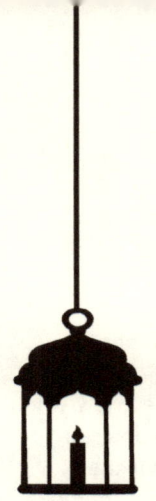

OTHER WORKS BY AMY CECILIA GRAINGER

A Philosophy of Hope

The Space Time Lives In
Emerging Through Time and Space

Selected Poetry Collections
The Timekeeper
Houses of Hope
Transforming Trees
Chemistry

CONTINUING THE INQUIRY

HOW DOES IT FEEL TO BE HUMAN?

Thank you for spending time within these poems.

The Timekeeper forms part of a wider body of work exploring time, hope, and human existence through both poetry and philosophy. While these poems approach experience through image and rhythm, the philosophical works examine the same questions through sustained inquiry.

If the reflections within this collection resonate with you, the exploration continues in:

>The Space Time Lives In
>Book I of A Philosophy of Hope

www.ingramcontent.com/pod-product-compliance
Lightning Source LLC
Chambersburg PA
CBHW030455010526
44118CB00011B/950